A Gift For:

Najukochań'szej Justynce

From:

Mamy i Taty

I'll Be Doggone

I'll Be Doggone

401 fun facts about dogs

compiled by Ken Beck and Terry Beck

BOK2029

I'll Be Doggone by Ken Beck and Terry Beck

This edition published by Hallmark Cards, Inc. under license from
Premium Press America

ISBN 1-887654-87-9

For more information visit our web site at www.hallmark.com.

Interior typesetting by Bob Bubnis/BookSetters

Second Edition March 2002
4 5 6 7 8 9 10
Printed and bound in China

Dedication

This book is dedicated to all the dogs we've loved before, the ones we love today and those we will love tomorrow: Koko, Flipse, Mack, Ebon, Buck, Fisher, Yogi, Cricket, Huck, Lassie, Rinty, Benji and Yeller.

Introduction

Wherever man goes, goes his dog. There are more than 150 million of the creatures around the world (dogs, not men). It must be because somebody loves 'em.

One thing that is for sure—they love us. Many cherished memories are linked with a favorite dog that was ever ready for adventure and ever loyal, no matter how else the rest of the world was treating us.

That only we humans could be as half as loyal to one another as our dogs are to us. Perhaps that is why it comes as no surprise that the word dog is God spelled backward. What better gift from the animal kingdom could He have given us?

May we treat our dogs with love, respect and kindness, and give them plenty of water in hot weather and at least one pat every day.

There have been hundreds of books written about dogs, the majority of them concerned with the raising and training of dogs and quite serious in nature, as they should be, but we thought that the average dog fan would enjoy this compilation—a kennel full of interesting and unusual facts about dogs, ranging from the physical world to the literary world and from Hollywood's celebrity dogs to amazing canine curiosities from across the years and from around the globe. We make no claim to being dog experts, simply dog lovers, but we've searched high and low for items to put in this canine compendium, and we hope you like it. In fact, you might want to share it with the favorite dog in your life.

1. "Heaven goes by favor. If it went by merit, you would stay out and your dog would go in."—Mark Twain

2. The phrase "man's best friend" comes from an 1870 speech by country lawyer George Vest, representing Charles Burden's dog, Old Drum, who had been shot to death. In one of the most elegant speeches ever given, the accused was found guilty by a teary-eyed jury which returned a judgement of $550 in damages instead of the $150 asked for.

3. The hot dog got its name one day at New York's Polo Grounds when a New York sports cartoonist overheard a vendor yelling "Get your red hot dachshund dogs" (referring to the shape of the sausage). After drawing his cartoon, he realized he couldn't spell the word dachshund, thus he just left the word out of the caption. Voila, hot dogs were invented.

4. A puppy is a dog less than a year old.

5. During World War I so many French golf caddies were away in battle that dogs were used to haul golf bags around the courses. The canine caddies' favorite holes? Why doglegs, of course.

6. Dogs are descended from a wolf-like critter, the Tomarctus, which roamed the planet 15 million years ago.

7. The first dogs trained to guide blind people were schooled by the Seeing Eye organization in Nashville, Tenn., in 1929. Morris Frank and his German Shepherd, Buddy, were the first team in America to break the barrier. The U.S. Postal Service honored Seeing Eye with a commemorative stamp, issued on June 13, 1979.

8. The Top 10 most popular dogs in the American Kennel Club's registrations are, in order of popularity: Labrador Retriever, Golden Retriever, German Shepherd, Dachshund, Beagle, Poodle, Yorkshire Terrier, Chihuahua, Boxer and Shih Tzu.

9. The Peter Chapin Collection of books on dogs is a memorial library to Peter, a black Cocker Spaniel. It was begun by his Rhode Island owners and now contains more than 3,000 books. The library is located at the College of William & Mary in Williamsburg, Va., and every book has a bookplate with Peter's mug.

10. How well can a dog smell? Put a drop of vinegar in a tub of 220 gallons of water and mix it up, then take a drop of that and mix it in 220 gallons of water. Some dogs can still smell it.

11. The Basenji is the only dog that cannot bark; it makes a high-pitched sound like a yodel. It is an African breed dating back to 4,000 B.C., and is used for hunting reed rats. The dog trots like a horse and cleans itself with its tongue. A Basenji was featured in the 1956 Walter Brennan-Brandon de Wilde film, *Goodbye My Lady*.

12. Dogs are mentioned in the Bible 44 times; 35 times in the Old Testament and nine times in the New Testament. Cats are never mentioned. "A living dog is better than a dead lion."—Solomon in Ecclesiastes.

13. British artist Sir Edwin Henry Landseer's portrait of a Newfoundland hound named Neptune fetched a pretty penny, $577,500, a world record price for a dog painting, at a 1989 Sotheby's auction.

14. In 1990, Bill Irwin and his German Shepherd, Orient, began a hike of 2,144 miles, from one end of the Appalachian Trail to the other. Eight months later they completed their little journey. Bill Irwin is blind.

15. The American Kennel Club, the chief organization of dog breeders in the United States, registers 150 breeds in seven groups: working dogs, herding dogs, hounds, sporting dogs, toy dogs, terriers and nonsporting dogs. The AKC was established Sept. 17, 1884.

16. There are more than 400 breeds of dogs. Take your pick of the litter.

17. In 1931, Toby the Poodle was left the largest legacy in American pet history, $75 million, by Miss Ella Wendell of New York. Lucky dog.

18. Only one dog actor played Toto in *The Wizard of Oz*. His name was Terry, a Cairn Terrier owned and trained by Carl Spitz, and he earned $125 a week for traveling the Yellow Brick Road, which was more than the Munchkin actors who were paid $50 a week.

19. The United States Postal Service honored purebred dogs for the first time when it issued four stamps depicting various breeds on Sept. 17, 1984, in commemoration of the AKC. The dogs you got to lick were the Beagle, Boston Terrier, Chesapeake Bay Retriever, Cocker Spaniel, Alaskan Malamute, Collie, Coonhound and Foxhound.

20. The dog who posed with the sailor boy for Cracker Jack packages was named Bingo. He belonged to the snack inventor's grandson, who was the model for Jack. Surprise.

21. Nipper, the symbol of Victor Talking Machines ("His Master's Voice") and of RCA, goes back to the 1890s when English painter Francis Barraud portrayed his brother's dog looking at an early phonograph. Now Nipper has a younger pal, Chipper. Both are Jack Russell Terriers, a breed growing even more popular today.

22. "A dog can't get struck by lightning. You know why? 'Cause he's too close to the ground. See, lightning strikes tall things. Now if they were giraffes out there in that field, now then we'd be in trouble. But you sure don't have to worry about dogs."—Barney Fife, 1963.

23. The Peruvian Inca Orchid, also called the Moonflower Dog, resembles a baby deer and is a nocturnal creature that doesn't care for the light of day or the hot rays of the sun.

24. Chips, a German Shepherd/Collie mix, was the first dog to be sent overseas in World War II and is the only animal in the history of the U.S. Military to win a Purple Heart, the Silver Star and a Distinguished Service Medal.

25. The Chihuahua is the smallest breed of dog. Weighing, on average about 4 pounds and standing 5 inches tall. It was first exhibited in the United States at the Philadelphia Kennel Club Show in September 1884. Big band leader Xavier Cugat rarely performed without his pet Chihuahua in his pocket.

26. The only Shakespeare play with a dog on stage as one of the players is *The Two Gentlemen of Verona.* The dog's name is Crab. What? No "Out, darn Spot?"

27. The Bloodhound, the doggy G-man, is the only animal whose evidence is ruled admissible in an American court of law. Nosey critters, aren't they?

28. The Latin motto "beware of the dog" originally referred to the Italian Greyhound, not because it was fierce but only as a warning to be careful of stepping on these frail pooches.

29. Despite no scientific proof, it appears that some dogs are able to warn their masters of impending epileptic seizures. In 1993, British veterinarian Dr. Andrew Edney surveyed 61 epileptic dog owners. Thirty-seven said their dogs responded during their seizures, 21 of them before the seizures, by barking, whining, howling, jumping up, going for help, licking their owners' faces or pushing them down and lying beside them.

30. Lord Byron wrote this epitaph for his Newfoundland: "Beneath this spot are deposited the remains of a being who was possessed of beauty without vanity, strength without insolence, courage without ferocity, and all the virtues of man without man's vices. This praise, which would be unmeaning flattery if inscribed over human ashes, is but a just tribute to the memory of Boatswain, a dog."

31. A New York advertising research firm conducted a survey of television commercials and found that four of the top 10 commercials featured dogs. Only one of the four commercials was for dog food.

32. The champion Greyhound Low Pressure (nicknamed Timmy) was the greatest sire ever with over 3,000 pups to his credit. What a stud!

33. There has been a National Coon Dog Cemetery near Tuscumbia, Ala., since 1937 when Troop was laid to rest in the woods where he had treed hundreds of coons over the years. "There's a coon dog heaven, and Old Red is there."— Bill Ramsay

34. President Harding had an Airedale named Laddie Boy who led the Humane Society's "Be Kind to Animals" Parade through the streets of Washington, D.C. After his death, newspaper boys across the nation donated one cent apiece; thus 19,134 pennies were melted down to make his statue, which is now in the Smithsonian. That's a lot of dog cents.

35. The Airedale is known as the "king of terriers" because of its size. It gets its name from the Aire River in Yorkshire, England.

36. George Tirebiter was a mongrel who chased cars at the University of Southern California campus in 1940 and who eventually became the mascot of the Trojan football team. In 1943, George was stolen before a USC-UCLA game, and when he was found, the letters UCLA were shaved onto his back.

37. A black Spaniel named Blackie was Ernest Hemingway's companion for twelve years. Ask not for whom the dog barks, it barks for thee.

38. The Doberman Pinscher gets its name from Louis Doberman of Apolda, Germany, who began experiments to breed the dog in 1890. Six of this breed co-starred in the 1972 film *The Doberman Gang*. Ironically, Mr. Doberman was a tax collector, and, boy, can these dogs really take a bite out of you.

39. According to the National Dog Registry of Woodstock, N.Y., an estimated 2.5 million dogs are stolen every year. The Registry also informs that twice as many dogs are lost on the 4th of July because of the noise of fireworks. It recommends that pets be tattooed for easy identification. For more information, call 1-800-NDR-DOGS.

40. Nine different collies have portrayed Lassie on screen and TV. All were trained by Rudd Weatherwax or his son Robert. All nine dogs have been male, while the Lassie character is a female. Now that's acting.

41. The rarest breed of dog is probably the American Hairless Terrier of which there were only 70 in 1988. There are even fewer Hairless heirs.

42. Dogs have four different types of stride, each with its own characteristics. The walk (right front foot forward, then left hind, followed by left front foot forward, then right hind, etc.); the trot (right front and left hind at same time followed by left front and right hind, etc.); the amble (two right feet at same time followed by two left feet at same time, etc.); and the run (all four feet at the same time). That's some feat.

43. The Dalmation, also known as the English Coach Dog, the Carriage Dog, the Fire House Dog and the Plum Pudding Dog, is born pure white. Its association with fire stations comes from the fact that the breed gets along well with horses, and back when fire trucks were pulled by horses, the Dalmation would run ahead of the team to clear the road. In ancient times, Dalmations were companions of chariot drivers.

44. John Wayne's partners in two of his westerns were relatives of Lassie. In Louis L'Amour's *Hondo* (1953), the Duke's co-star, named Sam, was Laddie, a brother to the TV *Lassie* who also performed Lassie's stunts. In *Big Jake* (1971), Wayne's dog was a direct descendant of Laddie. Wayne got his nickname of Duke because he had a dog named Duke when he was a lad.

45. The world's first space traveler was Laika, a female Samoyed husky, whom Russian scientists rocketed into space in a Sputnik satellite in 1957. That was one doggone dog gone.

46. Digswell the dog, a British astronaut, orbited the world in a Russian rocket in November 1992, before splashing down near Seattle. The stuffed dog is the mascot of America's Young Astronauts Council.

47. Hollywood really went to the dogs for the world premiere of *The Biscuit Eater* in 1940. Dogs of many Hollywood stars arrived in limousines and in tuxedos and were escorted to reserve seats in the front row.

48. For more than two years, Lady, a mongrel, wrote a weekly advice column for dog owners in the *National Examiner.* She also wrote a book, *The Gospel According to Lady,* and ran for the presidency in 1980 with the slogan, "It's better for a dog to go to the White House than for the White House to go to the dogs." Lady had a human secretary in Charles Stoney Jackson.

49. The highest jump by a dog on record, 12 feet 2½ inches, over a smooth, wooden wall, was performed by a lurcher dog named Stag in 1993 in Great Britain. Down, boy.

50. Hartsdale Canine Cemetery in Westchester County, N.Y., was established in 1896 and is the oldest pet cemetery in the nation, but the best place to bury a dog is in the heart of its master.

51. Wholly Mack-eral. The Mack truck symbol of a bulldog originated in France during World War I when English tommies and American doughboys gave the nickname "Bulldog Mack" to the chain-driven, AC model Mack truck. The blunt, snub-nosed hood gave it the look of a bulldog, and the legendary durability of the nearly 5,000 trucks shipped to France suggested the tenacity of the breed. The designer of the AC model later became president of the company. After he carved the original figure out of wood in 1932, it became the hood ornament used on all Mack trucks.

52. And now for a riddle: The quick brown fox jumps over the lazy dog. What's so special about this sentence? See No. 395.

53. The coyote's scientific name, *Canis latrans,* means "barking dog."

54. The Boston Terrier is one of the few breeds to be "made in America." It's been called the American Gentleman.

55. According to *Harper's Index,* the category that school children go to the *World Book Encyclopedia* most often to look up is "dog."

56. Roy Roger's famous German Shepherd, Bullet, is stuffed and may be found alongside Trigger, in the Roy Rogers and Dale Evans Museum in Victorville, Calif.

57. The Dingo is the only wild, meat-eating animal native to Australia. And how would you like that kangaroo steak, sir, rare, medium or well done?

58. The country is going to the dogs. Well, country music is going to dog food anyway, since country music legend George Jones lent his name to a brand of dog food, George Jones Country Gold.

59. The Pulik, a sheepdog, has been known to learn as many as sixty-five commands, while the average dog can learn about sixteen. When herding sheep, the Pulik will jump on a sheep's back and steer it back into the flock. Ride 'em cowdog!

60. Dogs were the first animals to be tamed by man. Or is it the other way around?

61. From signs on the side of the road in 1941:
    IF MAN BITES DOGGIE
       THAT IS NEWS
    IF FACE SCARES DOGGIE
       BETTER USE
    BURMA-SHAVE

62. President Gerald Ford's Golden Retriever Liberty (who gave birth to nine puppies in the White House) was so popular that the President sent out autographed pictures of the dog. The "autograph" was actually a rubber stamp imprint of Liberty's paw print.

63. During the Civil War, the Eleventh Pennsylvania Volunteers had a bulldog mascot named Sallie who accompanied the soldiers into battle. She was killed during a battle, and a monument to her honor was built at Gettysburg.

64. More than $6 billion a year is spent on pet food, and $430 million of that is on dog snacks. That's a lot of dog biscuits.

65. The Schipperke hails from Flanders, Belgium, and has been utilized in that country for many years as a guard on canal boats. Its name means "little skipper."

66. Pete the Pup, the Pit Bull of Little Rascals fame, was the longest-lived character in the series. The original Pete was born with a half circle around his right eye, so Hal Roach hired an unknown artist to complete the circle. The artist became makeup legend Max Factor. Pete is buried in a marked grave in Hollywood.

67. Bang, a Greyhound, jumped 30 feet, a world record distance, while chasing a hare in 1849. He caught it.

68. An Eskimo dog named Balto led a crew of 19 drivers and dog teams carrying serum 650 miles through an Alaskan blizzard from Nenana to Nome to save the town from a diptheria epidemic in 1925. The famous Iditarod sled dog race is in commemoration of this event. There is a statue of Balto in New York's Central Park.

69. "There are three faithful friends—an old wife, an old dog, and ready money."—Benjamin Franklin in *Poor Richard's Almanac*, 1738. Two out of three ain't bad.

70. United Press International reported from Cairo, Egypt, on July 4, 1961, that when bus conductor Ali Hassan refused to let Shukry Zaki, 15, board his bus because he was carrying a dog, he was bitten in the arm—by Zaki. The dog just watched.

71. National Dog Week is celebrated the last full week of September. The organizers' motto is "Dare to be your dog's best friend." October is Adopt-a-Shelter-Dog Month.

72. Snoopy made his TV debut in 1965 in the Peanuts special *A Charlie Brown Christmas*. Snoopy was inspired by Charles Schultz' own boyhood dog, Spike. Snoopy is now 50 years old (born Oct. 2, 1951) and continues to collect Picassos and fly a Sopwith Camel. There are even Snoopy amusement parks called Camp Snoopy. Good grief!

73. "The dog, to gain some private ends, Went mad, and bit the man. ...The man recovered of the bite, The dog it was that died."—Oliver Goldsmith in *The Vicar of Wakefield.*

74. In April 1990, Maggie Patterson opened a Doggie-Drive-Thru in Niles, Michigan, where she sold homemade dog biscuits shaped like cheeseburgers and french fries. Bet she got a lot of dog bites.

75. The Westminster Kennel Club of New York City stages the most prestigious dog show in the United States each February in Madison Square Garden. It has been an annual event since 1877.

76. The Papillon's name means "butterfly" in French. Its ears stick out in the shape of butterfly wings. French King Louis XIV almost always had his pet Papillon pooches included in his family portraits.

    King Louis: "That dog's just like a member of the family."

    Visitor to the court: "Really, which one?"

77. President George Bush's dog had a hit on her paws after writing *Millie's Book,* an autobiography, with a little help from Barbara Bush. The dog earned $890,000 in royalties before the taxman came

78. A house dog in its native Australia, the Silky Terrier has been used by poultry farmers to control rats and snakes. It's no chicken.

79. In 1993, there were approximately 53 million dogs in the U.S., living in 37.3 percent of the American households. We don't know how many men were in the doghouse in 1993.

80. Hanna-Barbera's blue pooch, Huckleberry Hound, was the greatest show in town when it became the first animated series to win an Emmy as Best Children's Program in 1959.

81. Since 1986, the U.S. Department of Agriculture has used a green-jacketed beagle brigade to sniff out foreign animals and plant pests at major international airports. Boasting a 90 percent accuracy rate, their motto is "Our dogs don't bite."

82. Since a dog only has sweat glands in its nose and feet, it cools itself by sticking out its tongue and panting. Then evaporation of water from the mouth cools its body. The exception to the rule is the toy dog, the Chinese Crested, which releases heat with sweat glands instead of panting like other dogs. Then there was Jim and Tammy Faye Bakker's doghouse featuring air-conditioning by Carrier. It was eventually sold at auction for $4,500. The Bakker dogs rarely used the 6-by-8 structure because of the rumbling of the AC.

83. Dog owners see doctors 20 percent fewer times than people who don't have a dog. Take two puppies and call me in the morning.

84. When Ulysses S. Grant was president, his son Jesse had a number of dogs that died mysteriously. When Jesse was given a Newfoundland pup, Faithful, the president told his staff: "Jesse has a new dog. You may have noticed that his former pets have been peculiarly unfortunate. When this dog dies, every employee in the White House will be at once discharged." Faithful lived to a ripe old age.

85. The first professional pet detective in the U.S., John Keane of San Francisco, bills himself as Sherlock Bones. His sidekick was not Dr. Watson, but Paco, a Sheepdog. Elementary, of course.

86. Those prints you've seen everywhere of poker-playing dogs were drawn by Cassius Marcellus Coolidge (1844-1934). Coolidge's first customers were cigar companies which gave the prints away. Later he signed a contract with Brown & Bigelow and hundreds of thousands of his paintings were transformed into advertising posters, calendars and prints.

87. You can send your dog away for the summer at Camp Gone-to-the-Dogs in Putney, Vt. Fees are $600 *per week*. No kids allowed.

88. "A door is what a dog is perpetually on the wrong side of."
    —Ogden Nash in *The Private Dining Room,* 1953.

89. Female dogs have 310 bones; the male has 311.

90. Terrier comes from the Latin word "terra," which means "earth."

91. Betcha a dog biscuit you can guess the game with a little dog piece that has monopolized the board game world since the 1930s. Sure, it's Monopoly, and folks at Parker Brothers unofficially call their favorite little dog "the Scottie Dog." More than 150 million of them have been walked around the block in the world's best-selling game.

92. The prairie dog is the only North American rodent that barks like a dog. Though not a dog, it's a pretty sneaky rat.

93. One trained dog equals 60 search-and-rescue workers, and a dog can carry half his weight comfortably in his backpack.

94. Actress Doris Day is well-known for rescuing homeless pets. One of her favorites is a little gray Poodle named El Tigre de Sassafrass. You may contact her Doris Day Pet Foundation at P.O. Box 8166, Universal City, CA 91608.

95. Rhythm and blues star Rufus Thomas was a dog man from the word go. Among his hit songs in 1963 and 1964 were *The Dog, Walkin' the Dog, Can Your Monkey Do the Dog,* and *Somebody Stole My Dog.* Well I'll be dogged.

96. Dogs are more likely to have a nervous breakdown than any other animal, possibly because of their close association with humans.

97. IN THE CLASSIFIED PAGES: Lost: Three-legged dog, missing one ear, blind in right eye. Answers to the name of Lucky.

98. George Lucas named Harrison Ford's Indiana Jones character after his own favorite boyhood dog, Indiana.

99. The first president, George Washington, was first among dog lovers. Among his canines were Lady, Mopsey, Searcher, Cloe, Taster, Tipler, Forester, Vulcan, Sweet Lips and Madame Moose.

100. Bosco, a cross of Black Labrador and Rottweiler, was elected mayor of Sunol, Calif., in 1981. He was also grand marshal of the annual Halloween parade.

101. A dogsled race was held as an Olympic demonstration program on Feb. 6-7, 1932, as the U.S. and Canada entered 13 teams. They raced 25.1 miles on two consecutive days.

102. Snow dogs like the Alaskan Malamute, the Siberian Husky and Samoyed can run more than 100 miles in 18 hours, while a four-dog team can pull a 400-pound load more than 30 miles in a day.

103. Owney, a dog who was adopted by the U.S. Post Office in Albany, N.Y., was so popular because of his world travels that he was stuffed and put on display at the Smithsonian Institute. Because he roamed so much, his postal owners put a tag on Owney's collar asking those who came in contact with the dog to write their location on it. After traveling all across the United States, Owney stowed away on a ship and visited Japan and China before returning home. He is now at the National Postal Museum in Washington, D.C.

104. Rin Tin Tin made the move from film to TV with his 1950s series *The Adventures of Rin Tin Tin*. Set at Fort Apache, Rinty's best friend was a boy named Rusty. Three different German Shepherds portrayed the TV Rin Tin Tin, and two of them were descendants of the original film star. Yo ho, Rinty!

105. The New Guinea Singing Dog, somewhat similar to the Dingo, is so named because of its singular howl, which is an undulating and modulating series of tones that blends into a swelling "portamento."

106. The ancient Aztecs believed the Chihuahua could guide the spirit of his master through the world of the dead, so the dog was put to death when his owner died.

107. The most profitable dog flick is Disney's *101 Dalmatians*, listed in the Top 50 films of all times by *Variety* with a box-office gross of nearly $1.5 million per Dalmatian.

108. The German Shepherd "General" of the U.S. Army was involved in 220 searches for narcotics from 1974 to 1976 and caught 220 people in possession of drugs, giving him a 100 percent arrest record.

109. Adult dogs have 42 teeth. That's the tooth, the whole tooth and nothing but the tooth.

110. The Shar-pei was once known as the Chinese fighting dog. It has very loose skin so that it can slip the grasp of a foe. Pretty sharp, hey?

111. Southern Illinois University's first mascot, the Saluki called King Tut I, is buried 50 yards north of the goal post in McAndrew Stadium. The mascot often inspired his team to score tutdowns.

112. The highest-ranking dog in the U.S. Army was a Bull Terrier named Stubby, who fought in France. The World War I hero shook hands with President Wilson upon receiving the rank of sergeant.

113. The father of modern psychology, Sigmund Freud, had a Chow by the name of Jo-Fi, who attended all of his master's psychoanalysis sessions.

114. Americans bet approximately $3 billion annually on Greyhound races. I'll bet.

115. The first recorded dog show took place on May 30, 1850, in London and was called a "Great Exhibition of the Pugs of all Nations." The winner was a real dog.

116. "It is hard to teach an old dog new tricks."—William Camden in *Remains,* 1605.

117. Puppies' eyes and ears open about 13 to 15 days after birth.

118. President Garfield seemed to love dog jokes. He named his dog Veto. He once heard Charles Dickens read *A Christmas Carol,* during which Dickens was interrupted from his performance by a barking dog, which practically brought down the house. Thereafter, whenever Garfield met a friend who had been at the show, he would bark out loudly, "Bow wow wow."

119. The Saluki is probably the oldest of all present-day breeds. It was the royal dog of Egypt, and the Moslems considered it a holy animal. Once trained to chase gazelle, it has been timed at 50 miles an hour.

120. The Pariah breed, found in Asia in northern India, is unusual in that when the dogs are young, they are faithful and tame, but as they mature, they leave their owners to live in the wild.

121. General George Armstrong Custer owned a pack of dogs, which at times numbered as many as 40. His two favorites were Turk, a Bulldog, and Byron, a Greyhound. Several of his dogs accompanied him on his final, fateful trip, and at least one of them is believed to have survived the Battle at the Little Bighorn.

122. "Happiness is a warm puppy."—Charlie Brown (Charles Schultz)

123. More puppies were born in Texas than in any other state in 1994. The Lone Star State produced 107,000 baby dogs.

124. Dogs are treasure hunters in France, where they have been trained to sniff out truffles, an expensive delicacy, especially when you consider it's just a fungus.

125. The great-great grandson of President Rutherford Hayes designed a royal doghouse, commissioned by the Washington Children's Museum, for Ronald and Nancy Reagan's Spaniel, Rex. Inside walls featured the framed pictures of the President and First Lady. Ronnie also had a hound named Lucky.

126. The most unlikely mating of two dogs on record occurred in 1972 in South Wales when a male Dachshund crept up on a sleeping female Great Dane, resulting in 13 Great Dachshunds with short legs, large heads and raised ears.

127. Spuds MacKenzie, a Bull Terrier, was spokesdog for Budweiser beer and starred in numerous sudsy commercials. He was a real party animal and made *People* magazine's best-dressed list in 1990. Spuds, whose real name was Honey Tree Evil Eye, died in 1993 of kidney failure. By the way, he was really a girl dog.

128. Move over Toto: A 4 pound Yorkshire Terrier named Sadie was sucked up by a tornado in Saginaw, Texas, on Sept. 13, 1993, and set back down two miles away. He really was doggoned.

129. The Otterhound, once used for hunting otter, has webbed feet that give it aquatic maneuverability. King John reportedly owned the first pack of Otterhounds in 1212.

130. The Samoyed of the Polar regions is one of the most powerful dogs in the word and can pull 1½ times its body weight with ease. Mighty dog.

131. Jim Henson's first nationally-known Muppet was Rowlf, a puppet hound dog who co-starred on *The Jimmy Dean Show* in the 1960s.

132. Saint Bernards were trained in the 18th century by monks at the Hospice of the St. Bernard Pass in the Swiss Alps to be used for rescue missions and guide work. They have been credited with saving more than 3,000 lives.

133. Anubis, the ancient Egyptians' dog god of the dead, was a man with a dog's head. As a sign of respect, when these Egyptians' pet dogs died, their masters would shave their heads as a sign of mourning. An Egyptian Hairless?

134. "A dog teaches a boy fidelity, perseverance, and to turn around three times before lying down."—Robert Benchley

135. The oldest known fossil of a domestic dog is 14,000 years old and was found in Iraq. The oldest American fossil was found in Jaguar Cave in Idaho and is 11,000 years old. Even in dog years, that's some tired old bones.

136. Similar to seeing eye dogs, hearing ear dogs alert their deaf masters to alarms, doorbells and other sounds.

137. Richard Nixon's dog, Checkers, of the famous "Checkers speech," helped save his candidacy for the vice presidency. In 1952, when Nixon was accused of accepting secret gifts, he defended himself of any wrong doing and told of another gift he had received, a little Cocker Spaniel from Texas, whom Tricia, his daughter, named Checkers. He said, "The kids love the dog, and I just want to say this right now, that regardless of what they say about it, we're gonna keep it." Presidential candidate, Dwight D. Eisenhower, vowed that Nixon would be "clean as a hound's tooth."

138. Johnny Weissmuller's famous Tarzan yell was actually a product of the MGM sound effects crew. They blended four different sounds: the howl of a hyena, the plucking of a violin's G string, the bleat of a camel, and the growl of a dog.

139. The world's richest dog is Gunther IV of Pisa, Italy. When his owner, Austrian Countess Carlottta Liebenstein, died in 1991, she left the mutt eighty million bucks.

140. Three-time world champ Ashley Whippet has been called "the Babe Ruth of Frisbee dogs." Since youth, Ashley has been dining from an inverted Frisbee.

141. *Hee Haw's* hound dog Beauregard was very difficult to work with say cast members. Instead of passing along punchlines, Beauregard passed along gas. The original *Hee Haw* hound, was named Kingfish the Wonder Dog.

142. Because dogs are color blind, they can only tell colors apart by recognizing various shades of gray.

143. According to *Aventivus Annals of Bavaria,* written in 1554, Hungary received its name from a mangy dog named Hungari, who had no tail or ears.

144. "Dogs are so evidently intended by God to be our companions, protectors, and in many ways examples."—Bertrand Wilberforce in *The Life and Letters of Father Bertrand Wilberforce* by H.M. Capes.

145. President Lyndon Johnson traveled, slept and even sang duets with his little white dog, Yuki, which his daughter, Luci, found at a gas station and gave her dad in November 1966. He was so fond of the dog, which he swore spoke with a Texas accent, that Yuki was allowed to attend Cabinet meetings.

146. The Newfoundland has webbed feet and a coarse, oily coat that enables it to swim in icy waters. Newfoundlands have saved many people from drowning.

147. At the Burbank Animal Shelter's "Paws of Fame" are the paw prints of many famous Hollywood animal stars, including Lassies, Benji and Old Yeller.

148. One Chinese emperor had more than 5,000 Chow Chows, while President Calvin Coolidge settled for just two at the White House—Blackberry and Tiny Tim. Wonder if they chew-chewed on his slippers.

149. To raise a medium-sized dog to the age of 11 costs about $6,400, and that's not counting obedience school or college.

150. Norwegian Elkhounds were the top dogs of the Vikings. Skeletons of the dogs have been found buried beside their masters.

151. Some Saint Bernard teams worked in groups of four to rescue victims. Upon reaching the injured person, two dogs would lie beside him to keep him warm, one would lick his face to revive him, and the fourth would return for help.

152. In 55 B.C., when Caesar invaded England, the Mastiff joined in the battles alongside the British. The Romans used the Mastiff to fight against humans and animals in the arena.

153. The Pekingese is known as the "lion dog" and was bred exclusively for nobility in his homeland. At one time theft of the royal dog could draw the death penalty.

154. "There is only one smartest dog in the world, and every boy has it."—Anonymous.

155. President Theodore Roosevelt had a number of dogs at the White House, including Sailor Boy, a Chesapeake Bay Retriever; Jack, a terrier; Skip, a mongrel; and Pete, a Bull Terrier. Pete sank his teeth into so many guests' legs that he was impeached from the capitol. Bully for him.

156. St. Anthony is the patron saint of dogs (and cats, boo, hiss).

157. An English dog named Help rode the rails for three years with this inscription on his collar: "I am Help, the railway dog of England and traveling agent for orphans of railway men who are killed on duty." In three years, Help collected more than $2,500.

158. When John F. Kennedy was president, his dogs were assigned the District of Columbia dog tags No. 1 through No.3.

159. All purebred Belgian Sheepdogs or Groenendaelers come from the original strain bred at Groenendael, a castle in the forest south of Brussels, Belgium. The dog was used as a messenger in World War I.

160. Tige, one of the funnies' first talking animals, originally appeared in 1897 in Richard Outcault's Sunday comic panel *The Yellow Kid.* Tige reappeared in 1902 in a new comic strip as Buster Brown's pet pooch. Buster and Tige later became trademarks for the Buster Brown Shoe Company and starred in their own 1950s TV show with little boy Brown saying, "Hi, gang. I'm Buster Brown. I live in a shoe. This is my dog Tige. He lives there too."

161. Pekingese were so well-loved in China in the 19th century that slave girls were sometimes used as wet nurses to suckle the dogs. In 1860, when Europe invaded the Imperial Court, most of the owners killed their dogs rather than allow the Europeans to take them.

162. The Portuguese Water Dog dives to retrieve lost nets and other fishing gear and can bring back fish that escape the trawl. The American Water Spaniel maneuvers through water using its tail like a rudder.

163. "On the green banks of Shannon, when Sheelah was nigh, No blithe Irish lad was so happy as I; No harp like my own could so cheerily play, And wherever I went was my poor dog Tray."—Thomas Campbell in *The Harper.*

164. One hundred forty dogs were trained five obedience commands in six hours and 55 minutes by trainer Will Markham in Coventry, Great Britain, on Dec. 3, 1989.

165. The word for dog in other languages: Spanish-perro; French-chien; German-hund; Russian-sabaka: Italian-cane; Chinese-goou; Japanese-inu; Polish-pies.

166. The Skye Terrier takes his name from the Isle of Skye where some believe it is a descendant of a dog that survived the wreck of the Spanish Armada.

167. President Harding once had a birthday party for his Airdale, Laddie Boy, and the invited guests were the dogs of members of Congress. The birthday candles were stuck in a Milk-Bone layer cake. No one knows what he wished for.

168. Since 1953, the University of Tennessee football team has had a live Blue Tick Coon Hound as its mascot. The present mascot, Smokey VII, like his predecessors, is famous for leading the Big Orange out of the giant "T" before each home game. However, the players must watch where they step.

169. The first hotel opened exclusively for dogs was the Kennelworth. Opening day was Nov. 12, 1975, in New York City. With 116 rooms in the hotel, rent was $10, $12, or $14 a day. Proof of distemper and rabies shots was required. No humans allowed.

170. Dachshund means "badger hound" in German.

171. Ken-L Ration has had a Pup Hall of Fame since 1954, and the Mighty Dog Hall of Fame opened its doors in November 1989 in New York City.

172. On David Letterman's first Stupid Pet Tricks stint, a mongrel named Mugsy grabbed a ton of laughs by sneezing and answering the telephone.

173. Especially beware of dogs in mid-June because that is reported to be the time to most likely to get bitten by a canine.

174. The Poodle is an excellent duck hunting dog and is unafraid to jump in any water. Its name in German, "der Pudel," means "to splash in water." Extremely intelligent, it is one of the most popular breeds around the world, and the Poodle is the national dog of France.

175. The Borzoi, more commonly known as the Russian Wolfhound, is a descendant of dogs that once roamed with Genghis Kahn. It was used by the Russian aristocracy to track wolves.

176. The Bloodhound is the grandfather of all scenthounds and probably got its name because it was owned mostly by aristocrats or bluebloods during England's Middle Ages.

177. John Steinbeck had a large French Poodle named Charley who was his companion as well as inspiration for the title of his book about his trek across America, *Travels With Charley* (1962).

178. The famous cry of radio and television's *Sergeant Preston of the Yukon* was "On King! On you huskies." King was the Canadian Mountie's intelligent Malamute Yukon King.

179. Handsome Dan, the original Yale mascot, was a White Bulldog and may be observed behind glass in the trophy room of the school's gymnasium.

180. American Foxhounds are descended from hounds brought to America by the explorer DeSoto in 1541 and English Foxhounds purchased by George Washington.

181. German Shepherds and Chow Chows are the dogs most likely to bite, according to a study done by researchers with the Federal Centers for Disease Control and Prevention.

182. The Boxer got its name for the way it fights and plays with its front paws. It was used long ago for baiting bull and bear. Put up your dukes, Duke.

183. In 1925, the Doberman Pinscher Sauer scent-tracked a thief more than 100 miles across the Great Karroo in South Africa. The crook must have been a real stinker.

184. The position of the dog's tail can represent as many as six different messages.

185. The Afghan Hound gets its name from Afghanistan where it has been used to track deer, hare and the snow leopard, but drawings of the hound have been found on Egyptian tombs.

186. The Bull Terrier was bred to fight other dogs, which was a permissible sport in early 1800s England. The White Bull Terrier is also called the "white cavalier."

187. One of TV's early dog comedians was Cleo, a Basset Hound, who made vocal observations to the audience, although cast members could not hear her, on *The People's Choice.* The voice of Cleo was furnished by Mary Jane Croft.

188. Champion Greyhounds can run faster than 40 miles an hour. That's no dog trot.

189. "Who loves me, will love my dog." (*Qui me amat, et canem moum.*) St. Bernard —*In Festo Soneti Michaelis: Sermo Primus,* 1150.

190. When Frederick the Great was interred at Sans Souci palace, his 11 Greyhounds were buried beside him.

191. The curious incident of the dog in the nighttime: "The dog did nothing in the nighttime. That was the curious incident," remarked Sherlock Holmes. Arthur Conan Doyle in *The Memoirs of Sherlock Holmes, Silver Blaze,* 1894.

192. A whelp is an unweaned puppy that still feeds on its mother's milk.

193. No kudos to Cujo. Stephen King's book and film *Cujo* was about a rabid Saint Bernard that kept Dee Wallace sweating it out in her car.

194. The Irish Wolfhound and the Great Dane are the tallest breeds of dog and may grow 39 inches tall. That's some tall tail.

195. President Rutherford Hayes had a pet Greyhound, Grim, who was run over by a train, causing Hayes to eulogize: "The death of Grim has made us all mourn. He was a great ornament to our house. ...The whole company knew him and respected him."

196. The Pit Bull is known as the Nanny Dog in England.

197. Comet, the Golden Retriever on *Full House*, exhibits such a wide range of acting talents that during the show's first season, he even played his own mom.

198. Two of literature's most famous dogs practically spring to life from the pages of Jack London's *White Fang* and *Call of the Wild* (Buck).

199. In 1961, Queen Ingrid of Denmark lost a pearl necklace while grouse hunting at the British royal family's estate at Balmoral. Later, a Collie Sheepdog, Gairn, sniffed them out. Gairn received a thank-you letter from the queen.

200. A golf course in Roaring Gap, N.C., is called the Olde Beau Golf Club in memoriam to Beauregard, a Bulldog. It is believed to be the only golf course named after a dog.

201. At the beginning of Disney's *Lady and the Tramp* appears a quote from Josh Billings: "Money can buy most things, but it can't buy the wag of a dog's tail."

202. According to the AKC the most popular dog names from registration records are Spot, Snoopy, Lassie and Pierre. The names Champ, Winner and Runt are not allowed. Meanwhile, a Purina Dog Chow survey found the five most popular dog names in the United States are Duke, Brandy, Max, Sam and Shadow.

203. Bobbie, a Collie, was lost in 1923 by her owners while on vacation in Wolcott, Ind. Some six months and 2,000 miles later, she found her way back home to Silverton, Ore. That's a doggone long dog trot.

204. The Akita is designated as a national monument in its native Japan and is so trusted there that Japanese mothers have left their children in its care. Helen Keller has been credited with bringing the first Akitas to the U.S.

205. Gen. Omar Bradley had a pet Poodle named Beau who was with him during the invasion of Normandy, on D-Day.

206. When composer Richard Wagner wrote *Tannhauser* in 1843, he had a collaborator—his pet dog, Peps. While composing, Wagner discarded every melody not approved by a bark from Peps.

207. For five seasons the Family Channel had a game show just for canines—*That's My Dog*. Humans were encouraged to watch the canine capers as dogs tackled obstacle course adventures.

208. In some parts of England, the Whippet is called the "poor man's race horse" because of its speed and grace, but 100 years ago it was mainly used as a rat killer.

209. By the age of four months, a pup can growl, howl, whine, bark and yelp.

210. The word's first successful heart transplant was performed on a dog on Oct. 4, 1956, by Vladimir Demikhov at the University of Moscow. The dog survived 32 days.

211. "His bark is worse than his bite."—George Herbert, 1640.

212. Possibly the largest dog funeral in history was held for Reveille IV in 1989. The Collie mascot of Texas A&M had 10,000 people at his funeral.

213. The Pointer takes its name from the Spanish who called it the perro de punta, "the dog who points." In this case, it is polite to point.

214. The standard Mexican Hairless dog is also known as the Xoloitzcuintli. The Aztecs named the dog after one of their gods, Xoloth. Here, Xoloitzcuintli, here boy.

215. Vending machines in Marin County, Calif., began offering Oops Scoops in 1989. For a quarter, dog owners could purchase a disposable cardboard contraption to carry their mutt's droppings from the ground to a trash can.

216. It is illegal to own a dog in Reykjavik, Iceland. You know what that means: no chili dogs here.

217. Before Rin Tin Tin, Lassie and Benji, there was Strongheart. The German Shepherd, whose real name was Etzel von Oeringen, was the first animal to star in a film when he made *The Silent Call* in 1921.

218. The world dog population is estimated at almost 150 million. That's just a ruff estimate.

219. "I think I have a right to resent, to object to libelous statements about my dog."—Franklin D. Roosevelt at a speech at the Teamsters' Dinner, Washington, D.C., on Sept. 23, 1944, after charges that the President's dog, a Scottie named Fala, supposedly stranded in the Aleutian Islands, had been returned home by a destroyer, costing taxpayers millions of dollars.

220. Dogs are very sensitive to vibrations and can sense earth tremors well before humans.

221. The Affenpinscher is a German ratcatcher. Its name means "monkey terrier" because it is small, black and has a face that resembles a monkey. Well, I'll be a monkey terrier's uncle.

222. When Herbert Hoover was running for the presidency in 1929, his advisers felt his image was far too cold, so they recommended that he pose with his dog, King Tut. Thousands of the photos were sent out across the country, and many believe the dog helped him win the election.

223. Ancestors of the Bernese Mountain Dog were brought across the Alps into Switzerland by the Romans. The Swiss used the dog to draw wagons filled with baskets to market. Git along little doggy.

224. The standard Schnauzer has bushy eyebrows, a full mustache and long, bristly beard. Called the "dog with the human brain," it can be found in paintings by Rembrandt and Durer. Its name means "beard" in German.

225. In Edinburgh, Scotland, there is a small statue of a dog, titled Greyfriar's Bobbie, which honors a dog's faithfulness to his master. Bobbie stood daily at his master's grave for more than 14 years. The story was turned into a film, *Greyfriars Bobby*, in 1961 by Walt Disney.

226. Eddie of *Frasier* fame, is a Jack Russell Terrier named Moose. He has pawed an autobiography.

227. The first dog racing track with electric lights was opened by Owen P. Smith in Tulsa, Okla., in 1920. The dogs were still the stars.

228. The Year of the Dog, according to the Chinese lunar calendar, includes: 1886, 1898, 1910, 1922, 1934, 1946, 1958, 1970, 1982, 1994 and 2006.

229. "It's been a hard day's night, and I've been working like a dog."—John Lennon, *A Hard Days' Night,* 1964.

230. Between 1802 and 1814, a Saint Bernard named Barry rescued 40 people lost in the snows of Switzerland's St. Bernard Pass. Barry was later stuffed and put in the National Museum in Bern, Switzerland.

231. The record for the largest litter is shared by three dogs: Lena, an American foxhound; Bootsie, a Great Dane; and Careless Ann, a Saint Bernard. They each gave birth to 23 pups. Cheaper by the two dozen.

232. The Saint Bernard is the heaviest breed of dog and weighs as much as two hundred pounds. Holy dog!

233. All dog species, except for the Chow Chow and Shar-pei, have pink tongues. Their tongues are blue-black.

234. There are about 450 pet cemeteries in the United States and 65 pet-death support groups.

235. One of the funny pages' most famous pooches is Blondie and Dagwood's Daisy. The dog also co-starred with her masters in a series of 1940s films. And one comic dog wears a uniform, Sarge's dog Otto from *Beetle Bailey.*

236. In Rodbey, Denmark, there is a Wolf museum called Lungholm Viveparik.

237. The Pharoah Hound blushes. Its nose and ears turn pink when it gets excited. King Tut buried his Pharoah Hound in a perfumed coffin.

238. A dog's height is measured to the shoulders or withers, not the top of its head.

239. The Sanford, Fla., police department isn't letting stray bullets go to the dogs. In 1989, they ordered bulletproof vests for their two members of the K-9 corps. The vests cost around $750 each.

240. The famous Iditarod Trail Sled Dog Race begins on Fourth Avenue in Anchorage, Alaska, and ends in Nome, 1,100 miles to the northwest. The race originated in 1972, and the course record of nine days, two hours and 43 minutes was set in 1995.

241. Lassie was created by author Eric Knight and made world famous in his 1940 novel *Lassie Come-Home.* Knight's real-life inspiration for Lassie was his own Collie, Toots.

242. *Canis* is the Latin word for dog.

243. An average of 10 mail carriers a day are bitten by dogs. Help stamp out dog bites.

244. Mystery novelist Dashiell Hammett gave sleuthhounds Nick and Nora Charles their own hound, a terrier named Asta. Asta also appeared in *The Thin Man* film series as well as in the 1950s TV series of the same title.

245. "No need to fear, Underdog is here" was the cry of Wally Cox as he provided the voice for this 1960s cartoon hero. Underdog was in real life Shoeshine Boy, and his girlfriend was Sweet Polly Purebred.

246. President Eisenhower had two dogs in the White House, Heidi and Spunky, but when Heidi urinated on the carpet, it was goodbye Heidi.

247. Bear, a black Labrador Retriever from Cord, Ark., was flown more than 16,000 miles after he got lost in a forgotten recess of a United Airlines 747 in 1974. His journey took him from Seattle to Chicago, to San Francisco, to New York City, to Los Angeles, and twice to Honolulu before coming back to his owner in Memphis.

248. The Cairn Terrier got its name on the Isle of Skye where it was used to chase varmints from cairns or piles of rocks used as landmarks.

249. Chesapeake Bay Retrievers are descendants of two Newfoundland pups that were on a British brig that wrecked off the coast of Maryland in 1807. They were given to rescuers by the survivors of the wreck as a gift. The breed is the state dog of Maryland.

250. The first animals to survive a flight around the Earth were the Soviet Union's Samoyeds Strelka and Belka, who flew the friendly skies in Sputnik V.

251. *The Shaggy Dog* in 1959 was the first live-action comedy Disney made. Tommy Kirk was the teen-ager who turned into the mutt because of a magic ring and an ancient spell *("In canis corpore transmuto")*.

252. Zorba, an Old English Mastiff born in London, England, in 1981, is the heaviest and longest dog ever recorded. He is 37 inches tall at the shoulder and in 1989 weighed 343 pounds. He was an 8-foot-3½-inch-long hot dog.

253. Taking its name from the sacred city of Lhasa in Tibet, the Lhasa Apso has long been called the "bark lion sentinel dog."

254. In 1926, Rin Tin Tin was voted most popular film entertainer of the year. The silent movie star is buried beneath a black onyx tombstone inscribed with "The Greatest Cinema Star," in Cimetiere du Chiens in Paris, France.

255. Named for the island of Malta, the Maltese has been a favorite pet of the rich and the royal for 35 centuries. Queen Elizabeth's doctor wrote in 1570 that the dog was much sought after, "for the pleasure and amusement of women."

256. There is a Bird Dog Museum in Grand Junction, Tenn., that highlights the talents of 36 distinct breeds of bird dogs, and houses the Field Trial Hall of Fame. The National Field Trials are held in Grand Junction at Ames Plantation, beginning the second Monday of February each year.

257. The doggy rhyme *Old Mother Hubbard* was written by a Miss Sally Catherine Martin. First printed in 1805, the rhyme goes back to the 16th century when Cardinal Wolsey had to jump through hoops to obtain a divorce for Henry VIII from the Pope. The 1805 toy book (3 by 4 inches) was so popular that by 1807 it was in its 24th edition.

258. The first dog show of note in the U.S. was held in New York City's Hippodrome on May 8, 1877. One thousand one hundred ninety-one dogs entered the contest. Barnum's American Museum sponsored a dog show May 8-12, 1862.

260. Most dogs have two coats, an outer coat of long, guard hairs and an undercoat of shorter, fluffy hair.

261. The first official Greyhound track opened in Tucson, Ariz., in 1909. I'll bet.

262. Japanese explorer Naomi Uemura was the first man to reach the North Pole alone by dog sled on April 30, 1978. It took him 54 days to cover the 600 miles. That's a lot of walkies.

263. Mike was the famous Border Collie who starred with Nick Nolte in the feature film *Down and Out in Beverly Hills.* You can see his paw print on the Hollywood Walk of Fame.

264. The Cocker Spaniel was once called the "dog for woodcock," then "cocking spaniel" and finally "spaniel." When it was brought from Spain to France, the French called it Espagno, French for Spaniard. In England, the word "Espagnol" became Spaniel.

265. Most Mexican Hairless dogs have no fur except for a tiny patch on top of their heads. But one furry puppy, a "powder puff," is born into each litter to keep the little baldies warm.

266. The Puli, a Hungarian sheepdog, has fur tangled into long, ropelike cords, which protects it from insect bites, thorns and insulates it from the heat. Herdsmen will sometimes spend a year's wages to purchase one.

267. Waldo on *Nanny and the Professor* was a psychic sheepdog that could telecommunicate with the nanny. Wonder if Dionne Warwick knew that.

268. An Australian cattle dog named Bluey lived 29 years and five months, longer than any other known dog, and was put to sleep in 1939.

269. Most dogs shed their hair in late spring and grow it back in the fall.

270. Queen Victoria kept dozens of dogs for pets, but her favorite was a miniature Spaniel named Dash.

271. The Byrd Dog Memorial Museum in Wonalancet, N.H., honors canines that were instrumental in helping explorers cross Antarctica. Pretty cool.

272. Cynophobia is the fear of dogs, but we'll have none of that around here.

273. During World War II, a black-and-white mongrel named Rob made more than 20 parachute jumps behind enemy lines while serving with the Special Air Service. Watch out for falling dogs.

274. From 1936 to 1953, the American Cocker Spaniel was the most popular dog in the U.S. The history of "Spanyells" dates back to the 14th century. They had a right to be cocky.

275. The Rhodesian Ridgeback, a hound with a characteristic ridge down its back, was brought to Rhodesia by a missionary and excelled at hunting big game. At one time it was called the Lion Dog because of its ability to fight lions.

276. "The yellowest cur I knew, was to the boy who loved him, true." Unknown—The Dog.

277. The Great Pyrenees is believed to be the most powerful dog in existence. He has been called "the great dog of the mountains" because he has long served to protect flocks of sheep in the mountains between France and Spain.

278. The Kennedy's dog gave birth to four pups, Butterfly, Blackie, Streaker, and White Tips, while in the White House. During a letter-writing campaign to find homes for the pups, one child wrote in: "I will raise a dog to be a Democrat and bite all Republicans."

279. Ireland's Kerry Blue Terrier is the country's national dog and was first discovered in the mountainous area of County Kerry.

280. The first animal kept alive with insulin was a diabetic black and white mongrel named Marjorie.

281. *Old Yeller* was Walt Disney's first film about a boy and his dog. The 1957 film starred Tommy Kirk and Kevin Corcoran as Yeller's boy masters. Spike starred as Old Yeller.

282. *Cave canem* is Latin for "beware of the dog."

283. According to superstition, a dog's howling foretells death, and dogs can see death enter the house of someone who is about to die.

284. The Pug is the national dog of Holland because in 1792 a Pug alerted a Dutch prince of oncoming enemy forces. Its name comes from the Latin word *"pugnis"* for fist. The dog's profile resembles the shadow of a clenched fist.

285. The smallest mature dog on record was a Yorkshire Terrier who was 2½ inches tall and 3¾ inches long and weighed four ounces. The smallest living adult dog is a Yorkshire Terrier named Summerann Thumberlina, who is 8 inches long and weighed 20 ounces in 1992.

286. Dennis the Menace's favorite mutt, Ruff, first appeared in 1951. One of the sheepdog's favorite hobbies is digging up good ole Mr. Wilson's flower beds. Little Ricky's dog on *I Love Lucy*, also played Mr. Wilsons dog, Freemont, on *Dennis the Menace*.

287. Hollywood star dogs generally earn around $250 a day for their thespian talents. That's 31 barks, err, bucks an hour.

288. Argos, Ulysses' hunting dog, was the only one to recognize the Greek hero when he returned home disguised as a beggar after being away for 20 years.

289. Once upon a time, the Greyhound, considered the nobleman of the hounds, could only be owned by royalty.

290. The President of the Confederacy, Jefferson Davis, had a favorite pet in his Mastiff Traveler. The dog was buried in front of Davis' house with an engraved headstone.

291. According to the book *Rules of Thumb,* a dog kennel should be two times the length of the dog, measured from nose to tail tip.

292. Since 1956, the University of Georgia football team has had a solid white English Bulldog named Uga as a mascot. Uga V now reigns, but his father, Uga IV, appeared at the Heisman Trophy banquet in 1982. He was posthumously awarded a varsity letter. All of the Ugas are buried in cement vaults near the main gate of the South stands in Tech's Sanford Stadium.

293. The French statesman Lafayette made gifts of dogs to the first five American presidents.

294. The expression "to bark up the wrong tree" comes from an American hunting term, probably referring to raccoon hunting at night, when hounds occasionally lost track of their game and literally barked up the wrong tree. "I told him... that he reminded me of the meanest thing on God's earth, an old coon dog barking up the wrong tree." From *Sketches and Eccentricities of Col. David Crockett*, 1833.

295. "I had rather be a dog, and bay the moon, Than such a Roman."—William Shakespeare in *Julius Caesar*.

296. President Harry S Truman lost the favor of dog lovers everywhere when he banished a gift pup, Feller, from the White House after discovering the young dog was not housebroken. He passed the pooch on to the White House doctor. Truman also had an Irish Setter named Mike.

297. The canine villain in the Sherlock Holmes case *The Hound of the Baskervilles* was a combination of a Bloodhound and a Mastiff with a muzzle of phosphorus. Dr. Watson's description of the beast: "A hound it was, an enormous coal-black hound, but not such a hound as mortal eyes have ever seen. Fire burst from its open mouth, its eyes glowed with a smoldering glare, its muzzle and hackles and dewlap were outlined in flickering flame. Never in the delirious dream of a disordered brain could anything more savage, more appalling, more hellish be conceived than that dark form and savage face which broke upon us out of the wall of fog."

298. The Great Dane is of German origin, was named by the French ("Grand Danois"), lived in ancient Egypt and Rome, and has nothing to do with Denmark.

299. The Bulldog, the symbol of John Bull (England's equivalent to America's Uncle Sam), went from bull-baiting to gentleman's companion. The dog got its name because it was used to fight bulls for more than 600 years in Britain. The sport was banned in 1935 as a bunch of bull.

300. In 1965, the Singing Dogs had a monster hit on their hands, err, paws, with the Christmas favorite, *Jingle Bells*.

301. Fido means "loyalty" in Italian, and there is a statue to a real Fido in Borgo San Lorezo, Italy.

302. In 1907, American Financier J.P. Morgan offered Clarice Cross $1,380,000, for her Pekingese, making the dog the most valuable ever. Cross turned Morgan down. He upped his offer to a blank check, but to no avail.

303. The Kuvasz, a shaggy, heavy-coated dog, gets its name from combining the Turkish word "kawasz," which means "armed guard of the nobility," with the Arabian word "kawwasz," which means "archer." For centuries, he was the royal dog of Hungary.

304. Neil was the ghostly Saint Bernard with a taste for brandy on the TV series *Topper*.

305. Thirty-six hours after a breakout from the state pen in McAlester, Okla., a bloodhound named Boston had nosed in on 23 of the fleeing felons.

306. The Cardigan Welsh Corgi arrived in Cardiganshire, Wales, with the Celts around 1,200 B.C. Corgi means "little dog" in Welsh.

307. Dog hairs can grow to a length of 18 inches.

308. The world's tallest dog was the Great Dane Shamgret Danzas who was born in 1975. He stood 41½ inches tall, and 42 inches tall when his hackles were raised. Down boy.

309. The first international dogsled mail left Lewiston, Maine, on Dec. 20, 1928, and arrived in Montreal on Jan. 14, 1929. Six Eskimo dogs pulled a 200-pound sled with a mail pouch holding 385 letters. The dogs covered an average of 40-60 miles a day.

310. From July 3 to August 11, the dog star Sirius rises and sets with the sun. Early Romans believed the dog star was responsible for hot weather, and that is how we get the term "dog days" for hot summer days. Hot dog days.

311. Newspaper columnist Lewis Grizzard often referred to his dog Catfish, who like to sneak drinks from the commode.

312. The English Pointer was so dedicated to its master and its work of bird hunting that a story is told of one who was lost by its hunter in the moors, only to be found a year later as a skeleton dog in position pointing a skeleton bird.

313. President Lyndon Johnson had two Beagles, Him and Her, who were made famous overnight after a photograph of the president pulling the dogs' ears ran in hundreds of newspapers. In his defense, LBJ said, "To make them bark, it's good for them." Him attended LBJ's inaugural parade. Her succumbed on the operating table after swallowing a rock, while Him was struck by a car while chasing squirrels.

314. Literally working like a dog, terriers were used as spit turners in England in the 1400s. By using a rope and pulley and putting the dog in a round wooden cage, its running power was transferred to turn the meat as it cooked on a spit.

315. The life span of a dog is generally between 12 and 15 years.

316. When novelist Emily Bronte died, Keeper, her Mastiff, followed her coffin at the funeral and slept at her empty room's door for many lonely nights.

317. The Irish Wolfhound has been used to hunt everything from deer, wolf, coyotes, timber wolves, wild boar, and the African lion. One of the most loyal dogs, it has been known to sacrifice its life for its master.

318. Their dog may not hunt, but they sure could sing. The Everly Brothers, Phil and Don, went to No. 1 in 1958 with *Bird Dog*.

319. First Lady Jacqueline Kennedy received a dog named Pushinka as a gift from Soviet leader Nikita Khrushchev.

320. The Weimaraner's nickname is "the gray ghost" because of its silver-colored coat and the way it moves so quietly and quickly through the fields while hunting.

321. When the Jetson's anti-gravity dog Astro plays fetch with his boy Elroy, he employs a rocket-powered pack on his back.

322. Elvis Presley went to the dogs with his No. 1 hit *Hound Dog* in 1956.

323. In 1983, Percy, a Chihuahua was struck by a car, presumed dead and buried in a grave in Barnsley, England. Hours later, Percy's pal, Mick, a Jack Russell Terrier, dug up Percy's grave, and it was discovered that Percy was still alive.

324. "When a dog bites a man, that is not news, because it happens so often. But if a man bites a dog, that is news."—John B. Bogart in *Frank M. O'Brien, The Story of the New York Sun.*

325. There are more than 2,000 dogs shows a year in the U.S.

326. The Bedlington Terrier hails from Northumberland, England, and bears an amazing resemblance to a woolly lamb. It's wooly coat bears no doggy smell.

327. Let sleeping dogs lie. "It is nought good a slepyng hound to wake." *Quote Troilus and Criseyde* by Geoffrey Chaucer (c. 1374).

328. When Mike Knecht and Tracy Hill were united in holy matrimony in Red Deer, Alberta, Canada, in August 1993, Mike's best man was his dog Bandit, which means when Bandit gets married, Mike will serve as his best dog. When Liz Wales of Glasgow, Scotland, was wed, her dog Sooky was one of four bridesmaids. We assume the other three were women.

329. According to Greek mythology, Cerberus is the three-headed dog with a tail of snakes that guards the gates to the underworld. One of Hercules' 12 labors was to capture this critter, which makes him the world's first dog-catcher.

330. The Australian Terrier, one of the smallest working breeds, has been used to guard gold mines in the Australian bush.

331. A 44-pound dog can bite at 363 pounds of pressure, while a human only averages 50 pounds pressure, and the strongest men can only exert about 160 pounds of pressure. So don't bite your dog.

332. "The old dog barks backward without getting up. I can remember when he was a pup."—Robert Frost in *The Span of Life*, 1936.

333. Fat chance: 40 percent of dogs are overweight and 40 percent of pet owners keep a photo of their pet on them. So what's the chance of an owner's picture being of a fat dog? Answer: 16 percent.

334. President Coolidge's dogs had the coolest names of all: his menagerie included Prudence Prim, Paul Pry, Terrible Tim, Boston Beans, Peter Pan, King Kole, Palo Alto, Coolidges and his favorite, a collie named Rob Roy.

335. The Labrador Retriever used to be called the St. John's Newfoundland. The breed was first brought to the U.S. by seamen aboard cargo vessels.

336. "If you pick up a starving dog and make him prosperous, he will not bite you. This is the principal difference between a dog and a man."—Mark Twain in *Pudd'nhead Wilson*, 1894.

337. Dreyfuss of TV's *Empty Nest* was a Saint Bernard/Golden Retriever named Bear, and his father played a dog on *Father Murphy*.

338. The Egyptians called one town Cynopolis, the City of Dogs. When the town was excavated in 1900, thousands of dog mummies were discovered.

339. Leeds Castle in Kent, England, has a collection of dog collars, some dating back 300 years.

340. "If he's the presidential dog, he will be treated like a king won't he?" —President Richard Nixon speaking of his Irish Setter, King Timahoe.

341. After a dog reaches the age of two, each year equals about four or five human years.

342. Buck, the Briard on *Married...with Children,* was really named Buck, and he dined from a crystal food dish, unlike his TV master Al Bundy, who never dined from a clean dish.

343. Adm. Richard Byrd had a Wire Fox Terrier named Igloo who went to the Antarctic with him and traversed the icy terrain in four fur-lined boots and a camel hair coat. He later flew with Byrd on flights over the North and South poles. He was obviously a Byrd dog.

344. Umm, umm. Frosty Paws, a frozen treat for dogs, is made mostly of whey, soy flour, and animal and vegetable fat.

345. The Lexington, Ky., police department had a bloodhound named Nick Carter who tracked down 700 criminals during its long and illustrious career. Book 'em, Nicko.

346. Human panting is the equivalent of laughter in dog language. Kinda comes in handy for when you tell a dog a joke.

347. Abraham Lincoln's sons, Willie and Tod, had a dog named Fido, a yellow mongrel, for a pet. When the family left Springfield, Ill., for the White House, Fido was left behind. A year later, Fido was stabbed to death by a drunk.

348. Dogs are digitgrade animals, meaning they walk on their four fingertips.

349. Movie star Benji was actually a TV star first when he lived at the Shadyrest Hotel with Bobbi Jo, Betty Jo, and Billie Jo on *Petticoat Junction.* Discovered at the Burbank Animal Shelter by trainer Frank Inn, Benji has grossed more than $100 million at the box office.

350. Surfing dog Rocky, a Shelty, has been named a California grand hotdogging champ for his prowess atop the waves. Hang 20, Rocky.

351. The popular 1970s group Three Dog Night took its name from a term originating with Australian aborigines. During cold winter nights, nomadic people Down Under would sleep with their dogs in caves, thus an exceptionally cold evening might be a "three-dog night."

352. "The more I see of men, the more I admire dogs."
—Madame Roland.

353. Mickey Mouse's dog was first referred to as Pluto in 1931's *The Moose Hunt*. It was then that he uttered the only two words he has ever spoken: "Kiss me." Pluto has had two canine sweethearts: a Pekingese named Fifi and a Dachshund named Dinah.

354. A dog's normal body temperature is 101.5 degrees. Hot dog.

355. During the 1970s, the U.S. Post Office in Hornbeak, Tenn., had an official stamp licker in Rex the mongrel. Rex normally licked off a role of 100 stamps at a time.

356. A human's olfactory area, the nasal membranes that detect smell, is about one-half-square inch, while the average dog's is almost 20 square inches. Our smelling stinks compared to a dog's.

357. Dogs can hear frequencies of up to 35,000 cycles a second, compared to human hearing of up to 20,000 cycles a second. So that's how that dog whistle works.

358. Dagnabbit, that Southern cartoon hound Deputy Dawg could never guard the henhouse from Muskie the muskrat. He was voiced by Dayton Allen, also the voice of Heckle and Jeckle.

359. Meriwether Lewis' dog, Scannon, a black Newfoundland, accompanied Lewis and Clark on their expedition to the Pacific Ocean and once saved his master from a charging bison. The buffalo's Visa card was long expired.

360. When Eleanor Ritchey of Fort Lauderdale, Fla., died in 1968, she left the bulk of her estate, including 113,328 shares of Quaker Oil stock, to her 150 dogs. By the time the last of the well-oiled dogs passed on, the estate was worth more than $12 million. All of the rich dogs were cremated, and Auburn University's veterinary school inherited the leftovers.

361. A dog's heart beats 70-120 times a minute.

362. Is your dog stressed out? You may want to read to him Jean Farrar's *Yoga for Pets*. After all, it is a dog-eat-dog world.

363. The nine breeds that bite the least:
> Golden Retriever
> Labrador Retriever
> Shetland Sheepdog
> Old English Sheepdog
> Welsh Terrier
> Yorkshire Terrier
> Beagle
> Dalmatian
> Pointer

364. In 1959, villagers in Chedzoy, England, didn't like the idea of the rector's Kerry Blue Terrier, Pet, coming to worship services. The bishop of Bath ruled that the dog could go to church as long as she was quiet and did not interfere with worship. After all, said Pet's owner, she is one of God's creatures and should be entitled to go to church, too. Amen.

365. Goofy first appeared in the 1932 cartoon *Mickey's Revue.* His original name was Dippy Dawg and he was first voiced by Pinto Colvig. Well, Gollee.

366. Sixty-seven percent of veterinarians say they have felt depressed after putting an animal to sleep.

367. Called the "world's most intelligent dog," King Arthur, a Labrador, can hold his breath beneath water for three minutes.

368. "Daschunds are ideal dogs for small children, as they are already stretched and pulled to such a length that the child cannot do much harm to either end."—Robert Benchley in *Cold Noses and Warm Hearts.*

369. King Edward VII of Great Britain had a pet terrier named Caesar who proceeded kings and princes during his master's funeral procession in 1910. He was at the head of the pack.

370. "Raining cats and dogs" was coined from the days in seventh-century England when, because of poor drainage systems, heavy rains would drown dogs and cats and their bodies could be seen floating down the streets.

371. Sir Winston Churchill had a poodle, Rufus Two, who slept at the foot of his bed and woke him up each morning by licking his face. The dog would never, never, never give up.

372. There is a Memorial Wall for Dogs in Princeton, Mass.

373. The mascot of Cumberland University in Lebanon, Tenn., was a bulldog named Rascal, who from 1931 to 1940 attended every law class at the school's Caruthers Hall. When the dog died, he was buried with ceremony beside the building, and a stone marked his grave. It read: Here lies Rascal L.L.B. Attended C.U. Law School 9 years, crossed the bar 1940.

374. In July 1980, a police patrol car in Hanover, West Germany, was put out of commission after a dog bit one of the rear tires, causing it to go flat. McGruff, take a bite out of that.

375. The 1955 film *It's a Dog's Life* was told from a first-dog point of view throughout, from the mutt's humble beginnings in poverty to his rise to luxury. It's been retitled *Bar Sinister* for video.

376. In World War I, more than 15,000 dogs served in the Allied Forces as guard dogs and messengers, and about one-third were killed or MIA. In Vietnam, dogs were used by the army to find mines buried up to six-feet deep.

377. Sandy, the original canine co-star of the Broadway smash *Annie!*, was discovered at the Connecticut Humane Society and cost his owner $8. A mixture of Airedale and Irish Setter, Sandy played the entire Broadway run from 1977 to 1983.

378. According to a dog IQ test developed by Kathy Coon, which measures a dog's mental acuity based on memory and problem solving, mixed breeds and purebreds have equal intelligence, and males are slightly brighter than, oh well, never mind.

379. Patti Page loves dogs with waggly tails. Her song *The Doggie in the Window* was a No. 1 smash hit in 1953. That doggy innuendo paid off handsomely.

380. Modern Greyhound racing owes its existence to the ancient game of coursing where dogs chased game animals by means of sight and not by smell. The first formal coursing organization, the Swaffham Club, was begun by Lord Orford in 1776 in Norfolk, England.

381. The first dog license law in the U.S. was passed by the state of New York on March 8, 1894, and was "an act for the better protection of lost and strayed animals and for securing the rights of the owners thereof." The fee was $2, and unlicensed dogs were to be destroyed within 48 hours.

382. Ludwig von Bayern Wittelsbach of Palm Springs, Calif., has his own American Express Gold Card. Ludwig is a Pekingese.

383. The Dog Museum in St. Louis is a fine art museum featuring a collection of more than 1,500 paintings, drawings sculptures and models, all of dogs. The museum also has videos of all dog breeds, and among its artworks are paintings by Landseer. Live dogs are not allowed.

384. The Nova Scotia Duck Tolling Retriever is unusual with its method of hunting in that it attracts ducks by barking and running back and forth on the bank, enticing the curiosity of ducks and drawing the birds nearer to the shore. At this point, the hidden hunter shoots the duck, and the dog then retrieves the game.

385. While most dogs eat only enough to satisfy their hunger, the Pug is a real chow hound who favors all-you-can-eat smorgasbords.

386. Elizabeth Marshall Thomas, who wrote *The Hidden Life of Dogs,* spent more than 100,000 hours observing 11 dogs, before penning her 146-page bestseller.

387. The Bouvier des Flandres was first discovered in southwest Flanders, Belgium. Now a true aristocrat among canines, it was once called "dirty beard," and has long been used as a cattle driver. Head 'em up, move 'em out.

388. The defunct Memphis Mad Dogs of the Canadian Football League had a team mascot, Alien, a black Labrador Retriever, who sprinted onto the gridiron to retrieve the kicking tee after kick-offs.

389. The world's most wanted dogs are Rocky and Barco. Mexican drug traffickers have offered a reward of $30,000 for the dogs dead or alive. The champion sniffers have detected marijuana, cocaine and heroin worth $182 million. Snag, a U.S. Customs Labrador retriever, has made more than 100 solo drug seizures worth more than $800 million. Give that poor dog a bone.

390. The Collie takes its name from an old Anglo-Saxon word "col," which means black. Most early Collies were black.

391. A true sleuthhound, Scooby-Doo lays claim as the longest-running doggy-toon in TV history. He usually beat out his human pal, Shaggy, for most of the Scooby snacks. Don Messick was usually on the case with Scooby, providing the dog's voice.

392. Tiger, of *The Brady Bunch* really showed out in the premiere episode of that TV series as he crashed his master's wedding while chasing the girls' cat, Fluffy. Tiger went on to play Blood in the 1975 Don Johnson film *A Boy and His Dog*. Tim McIntire provided the voice for Blood, while Tiger barked for himself.

393. Wessex was Thomas Hardy's Wire-Haired Terrier and was written about in three of Hardy's books. The terrier was a full-blooded terror who had two teeth kicked out by victims and was allowed to walk on the dining table. It is said that T.E. Lawrence was the only guest Wessex never attacked.

394. What are little boys made of? Snips and snails and puppy dog tails. That's what little boys are made of.

395. The quick brown fox jumps over the lazy dog uses all the letters of the alphabet and is used quite frequently by beginning typing students.

396. The Rottweiler gets its name because it's descendants, cattle dogs, were left behind in Rottweil, Germany, by its Roman masters.

397. Old habits die hard: Many dogs will circle a few times before settling down to sleep because wild dogs used to do the same thing to make piles of leaves into beds.

398. Dogs chew on grass to add fiber to their diet. Nothing like a healthy green salad to perk up a pooched pup.

399. "You think dogs will not be in heaven? I tell you, they will be there long before any of us."—Robert Louis Stevenson

400. While some American soldiers were wearing dog tags as far back as the Civil War, the metal identification tags didn't become standard issue for all branches of the military until 1907. An exhibit of United States Armed Forces dog tags are on display in the Armed Forces History Collection at the Smithsonian's National Museum of American History in Washington, D.C.

401. "When all the world is young, lad, And all the trees are green; And every goose a swan, lad, and every lass a queen; Then hey for boot and horse, lad, And round the world away: Young blood must have its course, lad, And every dog his day."—Charles Kinglsey in *Water Babies*.

CANINE CINEMA
Top dog films

Beethoven

Benji

The Biscuit Eater (1940)

Call of the Wild (1935)

Dog of Flanders

Dogpound Shuffle

Good-bye, My Lady

The Incredible Journey

Kelly and Me

Lad: A Dog

Lady and the Tramp

Lassie Come Home

Old Yeller

101 Dalmatians

Savage Sam

The Shaggy Dog

Skippy

Where the Red Fern Grows

White Fang (1991)

You Never Can Tell

More doggone information of interest to dog lovers

The American Kennel Club's (AKC) address is 5580 Centerview Drive, Suite 200, Raleigh, NC 27606; phone: (919) 233-9767

The National Bird Dog Museum and Field Trial Hall of Fame in Grand Junction, Tenn., outside of Memphis, was formed to preserve the history and joys of bird hunting in North America. It highlights the talents of 36 distinct breeds of bird dogs. The museum is open Tuesday-Sunday and closed Mondays. For more information, phone (901)764-2058.

The American Humane Society was formed in 1877 for the prevention of neglect, cruelty, abuse and exploitation of animals. Its address is 63 Inverness Drive E., Englewood, CO 80112-5117; phone: 1-800-227-4645.

The Dog Museum, originally located in New York City, opened in Queeny Park in St. Louis, Mo., in 1987. The museum was founded by dog and art lovers dedicated to preserving the best of traditional and contemporary dog art and artifacts. The Dog Museum is at Jarville House in Queeny Park, 1721 S. Mason Road, St. Louis, MO., 63131. It is open Tuesday-Sunday and closed Mondays and holidays. For more information, phone (314) 821-DOGS.

Selected References

A & E Monthly, June 1994

Animal's Who's Who, Ruthven Tremain, Charles Scribner's Sons, 1982

The Book of Answers, Barbara Berlinar, Prentice Hall Press, 1990

The Book of Lists, Wallechinsky, Wallace and Wallace, William Morrow and Company, 1977

Complete Book of the Dog, Angela Sayer, Gallery Books, 1985

Complete Dog Book, official publication of AKC, 18th edition, Howell Book House, 1992

The Complete Directory to Prime Time Network TV Shows, Tim Brooks and Earle Marsh, Ballantine Books, 1985

The Cracker Barrel, Eric Sloane, Funk & Wagnalls, 1967

Disney Adventures Magazine, March 1994

The Disney Films, Leonard Maltin, Crown Publshers, 1973

Dog Law, Mary Randolph, Nolo Press, 1988

Dogs, edited by Walter Fischman, Maco Magazine Corporation, 1964

Encyclopedia Americana

Encyclopedia of Medical History, Roderick McGrew, McGraw-Hill

Fact, Fancy and Fable, Henry Reddall, A.C. McClurg and company, 1968

The First Pet History of the World, David Comfort, Simon & Schuster, 1994

The Great American Candy Bar Book, Ray Broekel, Houghton Mifflin, 1982

Lassie: A Dog's Life, Ace Collins, Penguin Books, 1993

Leonard Maltin's TV Movies and Video Guide, Leonard Maltin, Plume, 1994

Mondo Canine, Jon Winokur, Dutton, 1991

More Strange Powers of Pets, Brad Steiger & Sherry Hansen Steiger, Donald I. Fine, 1994

Movies and TV: The New York Public Library Book of Answers, Melinda Corey and George Ochoa, Fireside, 1992

The Nashville Banner, various issues

The New Standard Book of Dog Care and Training, Jeannette Cross and Blanche Saunders, Greystone Press-Hawthorne Books, Inc., 1952

101 Questions Your Dog Would Ask a Vet If Your Dog Could Talk, Bruce Fogle, Carroll & Graf, 1993

The Only Book, Gerard and Patricia Del Re, Fawcett Columbine, 1994

People's Almanac #2, Wallechinsky and Wallace, Bantam Books

Presidential Pets, Niall Kelly, Abbeville Press, 1992

Readers Digest Illustrated Book of Dogs, Readers Digest, 1993

The Real Book About Dogs, Jane Sherman, Garden City Books, 1951

The Roger Caras Dog Book, Holt, Rinehart and Winston, 1980

Rules of Thumb, Tom Parker, Houghton Mifflin Company, 1983

The Tennessean, various issues

TV Guide, various issues

The Ultimate Disney Trivia Book, Kevin Neary and Dave Smith, Hyperion, 1992

USA Weekend, July 24, 1994

What Counts: The Complete Harper's Index, Harpers Magazine-Henry Holt and Company, Charis Conn and Ilena Silverman, 1991

World Almanac and Book of Facts, St. Martin's Press, 1994

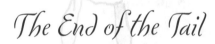

The End of the Tail